Broken for Assignment

The Beauty of a Broken Vase

Lorna Grace Sippo

The sacrifices of God are a broken spirit a broken and a contrite heart, oh God (Psalm 51:17 ESV).
I have become like a broken vessel.

WestBow Press books may be ordered through booksellers or by contacting:

WestBow Press
A Division of Thomas Nelson & Zondervan
1663 Liberty Drive
Bloomington, IN 47403
www.westbowpress.com
844-714-3454

ISBN: 978-1-6642-3610-3 (sc)
ISBN: 978-1-6642-3611-0 (e)

Library of Congress Control Number: 2021911044

Print information available on the last page.

WestBow Press rev. date: 6/28/2021

Dedication and Acknowledgments

This book is dedicated first to my Lord and Savior Jesus Christ, my Deliverer, who has loved me unconditionally and held my hand as I have walked this path with him. He keeps radiating in my life. I also dedicate *Broken for Assignment* to the memory of Rev. Samuel Sippo (my late husband) for the absolute support he gave me, demonstrating trust and confidence in what God was doing in me. My children Diamond, Ephraim, Esther, and Berachah always have been a large part of my experiences. I dedicate this book to them for their patience and complete trust in their mom's leadership as they followed the path, I led them on.

I am grateful and thankful to God for Apostles Moses and Nathalie Mukwiza, my spiritual parents, for their spiritual covering, untiring support, and spiritual guidance, which has been key in my life. I am also thankful for Rev. Gledy Wariebi's mentorship and practical directives in certain areas of my life. Finally, I thank Mrs. Pheletta Kayea for giving of her time to help with this project.

I am thankful for all of you who made this project a success and a blessing.

Table of Contents

Preface

Broken for Assignment represents an interesting piece of work that mirrors God's handiwork in the journey of brokenness. It moves from a position of being knowledgeable and brilliant to a position of trust and total dependence. It presents the realities and facts of life concerning how God's creative abilities break and then reshape a vessel so he can use it. This is part of my testament of brokenness. This book was inspired by the range of challenges that kept occurring in my life. Even though I loved God and was completely committed to him and his kingdom, there were seasons when I felt my life did not make sense. Nonetheless, I had a promise, on the one hand, and God's purpose, on the other hand, to fulfill, so I never gave up but kept on walking with God. I never stopped but pressed on relentlessly and tirelessly.

It became quite apparent to me that God cannot use a vessel that has not been processed. Is it possible that these turns of events were God's way of processing me so I could yield completely to his purpose for my life? The processing was necessary, and I found it a most difficult place to be, but gold can only be refined and become beautiful once it goes through fire.

There is a place of promise that you can never discover unless you are willing to go through the valley of the shadow of death and harvest a dimension in God; which is being willing to deny yourself, put to death your carnal nature and partner with Christ. Then you have authorized God to bring you to a place he prepares according to his divine plan and purpose. Everything relates to destiny. Nothing is wasted; it all connects to my divine assignment for my life, my family, my community, and my nation.

Thank you, Jesus, for the promise!

Chapter 1
Beauty of a Broken Vase

Our lives can be compared to a beautiful flower vase made of glass. Such a vase is magnificently decorated with extravagant broken pieces of colorful glass, and its colors are meticulously chosen so its beauty can catch the eyes of admirers. This vase has two purposes: to hold flowers and to look beautiful on the dining room table, in the living room, at wedding halls, in banquet rooms, in the bedroom, and so forth. The vase is used as a special decoration to brighten up the room. Vases display beauty, brighten the room, create an ambience of freshness, and provide for a graceful atmosphere. This sort of fragrance is exactly what God has created us to be. "For we are to God the fragrance of Christ among those who are being saved and among those who are perishing" (2 Corinthians 2:15).

Being beautiful is an ongoing position and also a timeless one. It is something that a person strives to be instead of something a person strives to reach. In other words, it is not a static position; it is a progressive and profound one. It is a kind of posture that displays quality, personality, and restful confidence in the aura that surrounds the person who adopts it. It consists of the presence of God. It is sensational and extraordinary. God's beauty created within us has one purpose: to make us function successfully in our assignment. However, that beauty comes in the form of brokenness. God will break you until your will, desires, and emotions conform to his own, which is something easier said than done.

Therefore, to fulfill our assignments, we must be broken completely; all of us must be crushed, emptied, and yielded to God. Breaking us brings out the inner substance of our souls and spirits, crushed and poured out before God yet perfect for Yahweh's use. It translates to divine alignment and surrender of a vessel that can be used for

God's purposes, a vessel that is flexible in the hands of the Master. The beauty that results is attainable through the process of crushing and breaking. "The sacrifices of God are a broken spirit, a broken and a contrite heart. These, O God, you will not despise" (Psalm 51:17). This is what God perceives as beautiful: our brokenness, and our submitting our hearts and spirits to his will. We should align with God's perception of beauty. Although we do make efforts in this area of our lives, the ultimate outcome is that "God makes everything beautiful in its time" (Ecclesiastes 3:11). Pay attention to his time.

For this beauty to be pure and apparent in our lives, God requires us to go through a process of brokenness. This is an inevitable phase that determines the value of God's beauty in us and how "God effective" we need to be to accomplish the purpose we were created for.

Nevertheless, when we talk about authentic beauty, we are referencing the beauty that comes from God's presence. From God's perspective, it is called processing. God must take us to the darkroom for processing. This is something we must submit to constantly and intentionally.

In the art of photography, a darkroom is the place where the film from a camera is developed and produces enlarged prints. It's also used to process photographic films. The darkness of the room allows the processing of light-sensitive photographic materials. It takes an amount of time for processing. Premature opening of the darkroom will destroy the beauty of the final product: the photos. Anything that is underdeveloped in the darkroom will be viewed in the light as blurry and will delay the original purpose. A blurry image reflects a premature destiny. Its unclarity negates the full purpose of God for your life and its dangerous. Also, it is seen as an unfinished product and will depict a picture that mirrors a half-truth and is unauthentic. Likewise, as vessels used by God, our processing must be fully completed if we are to function in our assignments. If it is not, then it will bring a great amount of disappointment that stings.

A wise word to us all: Don't bypass the development process in the darkroom. The consequences of doing so will be regrettable.

God has sustained his beauty within us. Although our physical features will fade, God has devised a way for our spiritual beauty to be maintained (inner beauty). Our beauty cannot fully break forth without the process of crushing and breaking. Therefore, I compare our lives to the remodeling of a clay vase. A clay vase shows the process God uses to produce a beautiful product. One of God's purposes for our lives is to beautify our environment with his presence and override our atmosphere with his beautiful fragrance, which brings transformation even to the various cultures we are part of (church culture, community culture, and family culture). God himself holds that beauty in place just like the flowers are held in the vase. This clay goes through the process of artistry. A degree of creativity must be used to create an unforgettable and transformative outcome. Jeremiah the prophet said it right when he described us as the vessel God is making of clay that is spoiled in the potter's hand. "He made it again into another vessel as it seemed good to the potter to do" (Jeremiah 18:4). The process is messy at some point, along with being hideous and unfathomable. It requires a lot of stamina and resolve on the one hand, and surrender and flexibility on the other hand, to create God's beauty, which can only be done by our expert Designer.

Chapter 2
The Process

Beauty is not attained. It is produced. How? It is a process. God's perspective on brokenness is that it is used to create beauty in the hearts of his children. His presence restores us and beautifies us. One only gets to understand and reflect true beauty after one goes through the process of being broken, cut, trimmed, and refined. Beauty demands the expert Designer himself to do the remodeling of the individual. His enhancements realized in the creative process of beauty is not what we have in mind. It is more rigorous and challenging.

Nevertheless, to get rid of the foreskin of our hearts, the dead skin of our souls, and to transform our souls and heal our broken bones and spirits, God's fire must refine us. We need God's fire because it purifies, toughens, and distinguishes us. As the cleansing value of the Word washes us, we also need the oil of the anointing of the Holy Spirit to soothe, heal, and empower us and flow through us. Water represents the Word of God, which cleanses us, heals us, and fills us up.

As believers of Jesus, we are required to be full of the living Word and give ourselves to meditation of the Word. The Word should be in our hearts, in our minds, and in our mouths. Only then can it work wonders in our lives. Being full of the Word is being full of Jesus and, at the same time, encountering him. It is a proactive state.

Oil represents the Holy Spirit, which cultivates the anointing of God upon our lives that drives us, gives us direction, develops boldness, and releases more of God's glory upon us. The oil of God is consistently used throughout the process. Its importance is related to our spirits, souls, and bodies.

But you have exalted my horn like that of the wild ox; you have poured over me fresh oil. (Psalm 92:10)

You have anointed my head with oil; my cup overflows. (Psalm 23:5 NIV)

Therefore God, Your God, has anointed you with the oil of gladness more than your companions. (Psalm 45:7)

This process is less than normal. It is demanding and ongoing. It requires patience, submission, and willingness. I remember when I was to take my twelfth grade national exams (advanced level). I had been walking with God while fully engaged in Scripture Union Ministry, just loving God and wanting to be with him. I had this amazing zeal about who God was and what he could do without any doubt. I did everything possible to be prepared. I had extra tutoring and coaching to hone my skills. I was very confident in my efforts and in my performance.

However, when it was time for results, I failed my exams. I was very disappointed with God. This was one of the markers indicating the process for brokenness had been initiated by God. My vase was not radiating much beauty. I was still confident in my abilities without the help of the Holy Spirit. Isaiah 5:21 says it nicely: "Woe to those who are wise in their own eyes and prudent in their own sight!" My vase was broken as my disappointment escalated. It broke into little pieces.

I was saddened and wondered why God had allowed it. I was all good with him. I prayed, read the Word, and was active in fellowship. I was embarrassed by the shame this turn of events would bring upon me, especially when everyone knew my fervency in Christ, which was a clear indication of pride. In Job 11:7, Job, from the depths of his heart, cried out, "Can you fathom the mysteries of God? Can you probe the limits of the Almighty?" (NIV).

It was unimaginable that I did not pass the exams. It was not making any sense. It was quite true that I had been adequately prepared and well equipped to take the exams, but still I failed. I never understood God's ways, especially the idea that it when I am weak, Christ strengthens me and, therefore, I should boast in my weakness.

My heart became offended toward God (that's not a good place to be). I realized I was going to be in preliminary year at university instead of intermediate year in the United States. This is the equivalent of freshman and sophomore years. You see, my being offended might have felt right and justifiable because I believed my success was the result of my efforts, not my dependence on God. In God's eyes, this is pride, which is hideous and does not reflect his beauty. So my heart needed circumcision.

The beauty of God is beyond our comprehension. God is so beautiful that his beauty overshadows any hideousness in our lives. His beauty is amazing. He does everything beautifully. Beauty for God does not reflect only in one's face, one's clothing, or one's overall physical appearance. God's ways are beautiful; his thoughts are beautiful. His plans are beautiful. His decisions are beautiful; his directions are beautiful; and his light is beautiful. When we begin to ponder on God's beauty, it penetrates every fiber of our beings. His beauty indicates his perfectness, grace, and glory. We experience brokenness so that God's beauty can radiate from within us. He longs to impart to us his grace to accomplish such a thing. Nothing is done outside of God's presence as he is processing us and as we let him run the program.

Amazingly, this cannot be done without total dependence and reliance on God. Being broken in his presence makes us open to his purpose and will. A better way of saying this is that God is beautifying us. We are hosting the transformer of hideousness; he is the beauty of all creation, and that beauty is manifesting in our lives. "Who in the heavens can be compared to the Lord? Who among the sons of the mighty can be likened to the Lord?" (Psalm 89:6). God's holiness and his beauty is beyond our imagination. It is a beauty that nothing can compare to. This beauty abides in his court, in his holy of holies. He beautifies us with his beauty.

My vase had to be broken into little pieces. If I was going to be the most beautiful, costly, and durable vase I could be, then I had to go through God's process of breaking me. This process takes place in God's school for brokenness. It is not pretty!

Chapter 3
Brokenness and Challenges

Challenges are part of the process of brokenness. They come with a specific intention and a desired purpose. They are sometimes from the devil, but most times God's vested interest is at play. God allows challenges for reasons best known to him. He is God; he is omniscient, meaning he knows everything. "I make known the end from the beginning, from ancient times, what is still to come. I say, 'My purpose will stand, and I will do all that I please'" (Isaiah 46:10).

Amazingly, as I discovered, even though the process may be rigorous, painful, and frustrating, this is one of Abba Father's requirements for brokenness. Its basis and foundation is love. "Greater love has no man than this that a man should lay down his life for his friends" (John 15:13).

It's a necessary pain that grooms a person for the process of brokenness. You know Abba Father will never hurt us regardless of what we have done to violate his trust in us or his love for us. He remains the same; he never changes and always beckons to us first with arms wide open. As much as he is a God of love, compassion, and grace, he is also a God of principles. In order to attain our highest level in him and accomplish his purposes, we must undergo the process of eradication of all the parasites that clung to us while we were metaphorically in Egypt. This method could be compared to what fasting does in our lives. It curbs the appetite of the flesh (when done sincerely) and sensitizes the spirit when God's face is sought desperately. Such is the case with challenges that are experienced while engaging in God's service. It's a way for God to announce that he trusts you and has selected you to be beautiful.

You see, promotion comes only from God (Psalm 75:6 KJV). When I was undergoing the process of brokenness, God was bringing me to the point where I could truthfully tell him, "You are my God. … 'My times are in your hand'" (Psalm 31:15).

There was a time in my life when I was deluded enough to believe that because I had a relationship with Abba (Father), I was guaranteed no challenges, not fully realizing that being beautiful, required brokenness: traveling light, getting rid of the excess baggage, attaining a new frame of mind, no longer operating on my own will, dying to the flesh, and showing complete obedience.

In 1997, just a month after I had gotten married, I lived in Sierra Leone, West Africa, at the time working for one of the largest and most influential international NGOs. I and my husband (who is now deceased) were pastoring one of the branch churches to which we had relocated after our wedding. We had such a harvest in our new home, including lots of blessings and much favor. We felt God was rewarding us for the faithful way we had been serving him. Yep, we were right about that, but things did not turn out in the way we imagined they would happen. You see, God works in unique ways he deals with the intents of our heart. What you do in his kingdom does not qualify you. In many instances it may even disqualify you and become your downfall when the motive of your heart is found wanton in his sight. God is the one who qualifies you, and he does this through the redeeming power of his blood, extending his grace and mercy to you not based on the works you have done. It is his grace that empowers you to keep going to accomplish mighty works in his kingdom.

In February of that same year, my husband and I realized we were pregnant. It was such a joy, all the awesome things that were happening. This joy lasted a few days, when I was thrown off by a severe bout of morning sickness. My husband thought it was a good idea for me to resign from my job since it was our first baby and because the church needed more attention and volunteers. I did not argue about leaving that job although it was a very substantial salary package, I was walking away from. Little did I know that God's hands were behind this decision as he was bringing me deliverance in an unusual manner.

In the month of March, the rebels hit Freetown. (Subsequently, they took over the country for nine months.) Their first stop was the international organization I had just resigned from. They beat up the staff, and destroyed, looted, and vandalized property belonging to the organization. Thank God that I had followed the promptings of the Holy Spirit. With that victory won, I had more fire to go through. That period was the longest nine months I had ever experienced in my life. Starvation, drought, and poverty all increased, each doubling in rate. Harassment was the theme of that regime—and I was pregnant! No doctors were willing to make appointments with patients. I started to see a gynecologist in the twenty-eighth week of my pregnancy. I vividly remember that I used to rise every morning and speak over myself and my baby, realizing that the days were evil and the times were bad. "I speak normalcy to you," I'd say over my oldest daughter, but not knowing at the time whether the child in my womb was a girl or boy. All I knew was that my faith was rooted in a deep trust in God to divinely intervene. Unfortunately at this point, Abba Father demanded a lot more of my faith.

Several days passed by. I had to eat rotten corn flour full of weevils that was used to cook porridge so I and my child could survive. I had to stay alive. It was very challenging. For the most part, my husband had to be in hiding because the insurgent government was looking for young men his age to recruit into their illegal army. I knew that God had not left me because of the strength I felt within. Three years prior, I had had the opportunity to attend a weekend charismatic Bible training school (FBTC).

It was the wisdom of God that was made accessible to me. In the second year of classes, one gets to choose one's concentration area, and I chose evangelism. I felt that this was the direction God was leading me in on my college campus. I loved going evangelizing, just sharing the good news of Jesus, his manifested power, and his love for humanity. I had a boldness that I know had come from my encounter with the Word, not just the Logos but also the Rhema, the living Word of God. It was as if a fire had been lit within me, and this fire gave me an unshakable faith. I had never seen the name of Jesus fail whenever it was called upon in faith. My unshakeable faith in him kept me going. I still pursued Jesus diligently. My faith in God was unshakable. I felt a sense of renewed strength that was not typical.

At one point, when my family started facing personal harassment, such as the rebels holding us at gunpoint and forcefully snatching our groceries, I started to question God: "God, did you really send us here?" I would pray and ask God to avert the war, saying that because my husband and I served him and were doing a great job where we were pastoring, we should be spared this sort of trouble. My inner thought was that this war would not happen because I had been praying against it. Another point of persuasion I used was to say that the church members were fasting and offering up prayers, so God had to listen to us. But I learned that God's ways are not our ways; he is always fully in charge regardless of the outcome. There are some things he will avert, but there are some fires he will let a person walk through because, in doing so, the individual will come out refined, being now purer and much stronger than he or she was when first going in for God's predestined assignment for his or her life.

As the days passed, the situation became unbearable. It dawned on me that the war was far from being over. People were being shot at for tuning into the government channel on the radio as it was mandatory to listen to the rebel radio station. Our electric power was totally disconnected. It was scary thinking how I was going to have my baby. With all the horrendous things occurring, it was difficult to find out if all this was God's plan. I pushed my faith into another gear, which was necessary as I realized that this battle was one of life-and-death. I could either believe God beyond a shadow of a doubt or be recruited by the spirit of doubt, which would do nothing but invade my life and kill me.

Amid all the craziness in Sierra Leone, I could not figure out what God was doing. It appeared that God was stretching me and developing a warrior spirit within me, one of endurance and stamina, one that could pull me through anything. I had questions about the chaos and the pain. Was God allowing this to happen?

But then there came the day for a bigger test, September 14. You see, brokenness also comes with crazy faith and confidence in God—nothing less. One must have total confidence in God that one will get through the process. This is known as total surrender.

I had to deliver my baby. It happened suddenly that my water broke at what I believed to be the wrong time, but it was right in God's time. I say the wrong time because curfew was at six o'clock in the evening. The rebel soldiers were already marauding everywhere, on every street corner. I knew the difficulties that lay ahead, but I also knew that the God of the difficulties had reason to allow this.

Amazingly, I had no fear. I wished God had opened my eyes to behold the armies of angels leading me on—I could not see them, but I could feel them—as my husband and I safely made our way to the military hospital, which was the only functioning hospital open at that time. It was a chaotic scene. There was shelling and bombing from government soldiers from the sea because the country was under an embargo for food and supplies. We had an illegal government that was not recognized by the international community. At this point, a ship was trying to violate the embargo, and the infraction was reciprocated with bombing and shelling from the ECOMOG forces (Combined West African Army Forces). It was terrifying. We could see the mortars lighting up and falling all over the area. It was amid this atmosphere that I had to deliver my baby.

At the hospital, everyone was in military gear. It was my first experience with childbirth, so I did not know what to expect. My confidence was in God, and I believed that his right arm would save me. It's amazing what goes through one's mind when one is in the midst of a trial. If this happens to you, you must understand that it's just a testing time that will pass. Refrain from seeing only the impossibilities of the circumstance. In the hospital, my mind was blank, but my mouth was speaking the name of Jesus! On my way to the birthing center, I saw about a dozen newborn babies lined up along the hallway. I came to learn later that these were dead babies. I had thought they were sleeping babies.

Calling on Jesus, I went to the labor ward with no doctor, just two clueless nurses who couldn't get my gynecologist to come in because the rebels had the roads blocked. I believe Jesus was in that room with me. Feeling the bold presence of God, I had no fear! Consequently, that presence I felt enabled me to safely deliver my daughter. She was alive. I was exhausted, but God's presence kept me going. He delivered me from high fever and other complications. The persistent shelling and the bombing continued. It was not going to stop, but I'd had my baby. Thank you, Jesus.

At this point, I realized the realities of being tested by fire are not the usual things we confront at church. I was high-minded and thought I knew the Lord, and I understood spiritual things. Or so I thought. Clearly, I was mistaken. Remember, God's ways are not our ways of doing things. One must be tested in the fire to come forth as pure gold. Gold to be purified goes through the hottest of fires.

As my challenges increased, I was constantly in war mode. My mom had asked me to move back into her home since it was my first baby. She felt that I and my baby would be much safer with her. I later discovered that my mom's new neighbors were rebels from the insurgent fighting group, yet God's presence was still there, giving me confidence.

Two weeks after my daughter's birth, the demonic madness among the rebels was at an elevated level. They would engage in rapid-fire shootouts from six o'clock to ten o'clock in the evening, shooting indiscriminately. My mum, aunty and my daughter were all lying on the floor, which seemed to be a good way of protecting ourselves from bullets. It was very scary, yet I held onto God. He was teaching me how to trust him, solely depend on him, endure difficulty, and learn perseverance. You see, there are three stages to the process of development. It starts off with patience, which is defined as "the capacity to accept or tolerate suffering or trouble without getting angry or upset." It then develops into endurance, which is defined as "the power of enduring a difficult process or situation without giving way." Then perseverance is birth. Perseverance is defined as "persistence in doing something despite the difficulties and delay in achieving success." Thus, one's capacity (dimension), power (authority and influence), and persistence (tenacity) all have to do with one's physical, mental, and spiritual state. All three traits have to be subjected to the process if they are to align with God's heart.

God has never done anything with me that is normal. This has just been a pattern throughout my life. Life has never been normal, usual, or ordinary. I came to realize that very late in my life. Many highly abnormal incidents have occurred in my life that indicate the sovereignty of God. It occurs to me again that God does a thorough job; he never leaves his work incomplete. Many times when going through a challenge I have trusted him to make it go away; however, he just energized me to go through it.

Another incident of brokenness occurred after I had graduated with my bachelor's degree. I was on the hunt searching for NGO job, specifically, an international NGO. I spent a year at home, while every one of my friends had a great job. I fasted, prayed, and stayed true to what I believed to be the steps to finding a suitable job. I was very practical about it, exhausting all the steps I had written in my notes from Bible study. I followed the instructions and was full of faith, but nothing happened!

To make matters worse, I would receive calls telling me I had gotten desirable jobs, but then two days after being hired, I was removed from the list. I was wondering what was going on. Was God not seeing? Did he not care? Or perhaps I was doing something very wrong. I felt God was really pushing my limits.

What I did not realize at the time was that I had overlooked the job God had for me that season because I was still being processed. A brand-new Christian radio station had offer me a position as a broadcaster, but the salary package was unattractive. I also thought I deserved to have my dream job, whereas this position didn't even come close. I was very reluctant and also ignored the voice of God under the guise of *I don't think this is what God is offering me.* However, I was stranded and felt very despondent, so I took the opportunity that was open to me to work at a Christian radio station. Thus, God's hand was very much part of this action. God was trying to send me on a journey of coming to understand the role of media and evangelism in the kingdom.

My new job brought back memories of my days on the evangelism team. I was involved in street preaching at the center of the city and the bus station. However, I could not fully figure out what that season was about. What I did realize, though, was that God was still trying to teach me to hear his voice. He was challenging me to determine how obedient I would be to following his voice when on the assignment he had given me, whether it was In a secular office or part of the kingdom. In God's eyes, my new job was my pulpit to touch others and influence them. So I recognized this same feeling that always occurs when I am in transition to a new assignment. The Lord was pointing out how he was going to make me a voice for him, showing me that it was going to involve my being on the airwaves declaring the name of Jesus and encouraging the hearts of those I was speaking to. I learned that the purpose of a job is not only to receive wages but also to serve as an open door for God to glorify himself and to use me as his voice, which was a humbling revelation for me.

The two years I spent at the Christian station, I developed a greater sense of the value of broken people and what it means to touch lives and bring hope to my community. I was so broken that I did not have time to think about my qualifications or the unfairness of my not having a job. At this point, I was in the mode of "Yes, Lord."

After two years, God started manifesting himself to me in ways I had never experienced before. I was interviewed for an accounting job for which I was underqualified. All the qualified candidates had been eliminated, and I was given special training for the job. Brokenness and obedience had aligned my will with God's and taught me how to trust God more. Two years later, I landed a higher-paying job with no interviews. It was a very high-ranking position. I knew God had been very much involved in the process of my getting this job. You see, I discovered that anytime a person's life is interrupted by either a tragedy or an undeniable setback, God has started the process of brokenness for that person. This process always happens before a great elevation or promotion. Evidently, God needs us to be well prepared to enter every season of our lives. So, brokenness breaks us out of our old selves so that we may move into these great seasons. Each season, regardless of the challenges it brings, should reflect God's beauty within us.

Everything that God had used in my life that I simultaneously depended on, God removed so I could trust him completely. He is always removing the old and establishing the new. The blessings of God restore my status as I am moved from lost to found. At this time of my life, even though fear of failure was all around me, I knew I had to break through with the Spirit of God upon me.

Again, my Father keeps reminding me that my total dependence is on him and that he is my reward. All the people I thought were my friends abandoned me during this period. Abba Father has a way of reminding me of my position in relation to him. Never before in my life have I felt the way I do now, because now I understand that these things God does are part of a process indeed!

Chapter 4
The Pathway to Elevation

Elevation comes from God. It does not come from the east or the west. It does not come because of our efforts and our accomplishments. It is a God setup, a God-principled system that cannot be bypassed. A person's efforts can only take the person so far because we are all limited and restricted. However, one may be elevated, with elevation being considered as an upliftment, a promotion that comes from God. It derives from exploring God's nature of trust and, at the same time, draws from God's unlimited river of sustenance. "With joy shall you draw water out of the wells of salvation" (Isaiah 12:3). This water becomes a refresher in your season of brokenness. It is an unending resource if you know how to draw from it. The woman at the well asked, "Sir, you have nothing to draw with and the well is deep. Where then do you get the living water?" (John 4:12). She was dialoguing with the living water but had not yet experienced the revelation of how to access the living water. That wouldn't come until she had an encounter with the living water. Jesus said to her, "I who speak to you am He."

On the pathway to elevation, one must go through the process of brokenness. During this process, one becomes enlightened and awakened to the living water. Jesus is a necessity in the valley of brokenness only because he refreshes us. That is how we survive our process.

Joseph's journey in the book of Genesis serves an interesting story of one's pathway to elevation. However, before being elevated, Joseph had to experience this process of brokenness. It could not be avoided. His dreams were overwhelming, and he could not process the real reason for the strong challenges he was facing. He had to endure the pain of God's breaking him and preparing him for his destiny. Joseph was naive, very enthusiastic, kindhearted, and focused on the literary meaning of his dreams. He did not consider it spiritual significance and was insensitive to his surroundings, whether they could breed dreams or kill dreams. He was sold into slavery, sent to Potiphar's house, and then sent to prison. Part of the road to brokenness for Joseph was his developing his skills for his divine assignment. It was lonely and cold, but such is God's method. Joseph had to travel this path to eradicate all that could hinder him from arriving at his final destination.

The valuable lessons Joseph learned in prison were a necessity for his destiny, part of which assignment was to reflect God's perfect beauty. The time he served in prison entailed not just physical confinement but also spiritual confinement, the purpose of which was to prepare him for God's divine assignment with reference to a nation, a people, a tribe, and a tongue. In other words, God's beauty is shown here to be not just for an individual but also for nations. Joseph understood the significance of his dream, but he was clueless of any deeper meaning attached to this dream. He was a prisoner of destiny, tied to a God-projected moment.

I realize that those who are walking the road of elevation tend to be prisoners of God's opportunities. Their future may be bright for such people, yet they live in darkness. They are carrying the blessing, yet they live like victims. They may be living in tents, but they carry the promise. You might ask me, then, What is the problem? The problem is the process; without the process, the promise cannot be attained, so therefore elevation is not guaranteed.

Elevation comes only after one has been tried and tested, and proven by God's standard, not humankind's. God calls all, but few are chosen for this special assignment. It is not an assignment to display pride and arrogance; rather, it is the seat of grace and humility, meaning that one is selected not because one qualifies but because God qualifies the individuals. It's just like the navy SEALs who are selected for special assignments and operations, the only difference being that they are assigned. Those who are undergoing the process do not make the choice of where they will carry out their operations; they are sent where they are needed, having been selected by Abba Father himself. It is a costly project that comes with one objective: having a successful mission.

The road up to elevation is really the road downward toward brokenness. Every path leads downward, and turning to God in humility during such times produces a servanthood effect in us. It is a position of learning, thoughtfulness, and revelation.

When I was working on my bachelor's degree, I was part of the university's Christian fellowship. This was a powerful group of students who were just sold out for God. We had a peculiar anointing; our passion was to see the power of the gospel be made known to the whole university and beyond the university campus.

During this season, I considered myself spiritually mature. I was part of the executive board, which was the spiritual team that led the group. God has a way of handling things and fixing us up when we need help to overcome our own ignorance and pride. Our executive board had a leadership retreat, which evidently was the time to bring correction to me. I was struggling with anger and did not know that my anger was spinning out of control and manifesting in my interactions with my colleagues in the Christian group. When this was brought up in the retreat, I could not handle it. I walked away from the gathering and went to my own room. I was embarrassed and was in denial. My weakness had been confronted, so that stronghold within me was challenged. I was in torment throughout the night. My colleagues tried to reach out to me in love, which, given that I was so adamant in separating myself, surprised me.

Throughout the night I slept not a wink. God was working in my heart. I began to feel warmth as he was talking to me about surrendering completely to him. In the morning, as my colleagues gathered, I was very embarrassed, but I stepped out of my room anyway. They received me in love, and we worked through the issues. There was an amazing atmosphere with God's warmth as they embraced me and counseled me. I felt this newness entering my heart and God's love melting my heart. I had feared being rebuked and rejected even though I knew something was wrong in that area of my life; I was dealing with anger issues. It slowly started to make sense to me that God was pruning me as a vinedresser prunes the branches of the vine.

At this particular time, my life was about avoiding stunted growth and clearing the path for my potential growth. The pruning did a lot for me. I left the retreat with a more teachable spirit for my journey. God had taken something old from my heart and given me something new. It was very good, so I thought I had gotten a new heart, that a spiritual surgery had been done.

For one to understand what brokenness means, God must circumcise one's heart and one's self-absorbed thoughts and, most times, interrupt one's meaningful plans. These elements must be attended to if one is going to be effective in the assignment God has given. I had been sabotaging myself as a reformer because even though I was passionate, I did not quite understand my position.

Brokenness to me means complete surrender, heart circumcision, and servanthood. God uses different methods to ensure that one is broken before one may experience elevation. The woman with the issue of blood in the book of Luke confronted this brokenness. She had spent all she had in terms of money and had consulted with doctors to try to find healing, but everything had failed. Her processing came in the form of trying her faith. Her problem was beyond the realm of not doing anything. Her faith grabbed Jesus's attention, but the road to this grabbing was full of brokenness. She lost her dignity, her pride, and her status. Even after her death, she has remained a model of faith for the world, but it cost her dignity and her resources. What will God's processing cost you? The story of the woman with the issue of the blood has been told for generations. She was known as a woman of faith. As a result, after being challenged, she received the beauty of healing.

Chapter 5
Promise and Prison

We cannot discuss the promise and prison without mentioning Joseph, especially the part of his story appearing in Genesis 39. Joseph fits the profile of being broken on his way to elevation. The scriptures tell us that God was with Joseph. It is necessary to know that when God breaks us, he never leaves us; he is right there with us much more than we know. This is key for us as children of God to get a strong grasp on this truth and believe it so we can depend on God's grace and wisdom throughout these seasons.

The scripture goes further, saying that God made Joseph prosperous when Potiphar bought him from the Ishmaelite. Joseph was bought as a slave or a servant, but he was highly blessed and very prosperous. This blessing was detected by Potiphar, who might have said to himself, "I have never had as much wealth or favor as I have had since Joseph stepped foot in my house." Potiphar might have also recognized that Joseph was Hebrew and carried the blessings of Yahweh. Because of this fact, Potiphar was very wise to turn over his entire household to Joseph. He recognized the blessing and was tapping into it indirectly. All this time Joseph was a candidate for elevation, yet his journey and pathways consisted of unusual challenges, obstacles, and abandonment, which is God's recipe for brokenness. Even though Joseph had made godly choices in Potiphar's home, he still went to prison.

Partnering with heaven requires total brokenness. God's pattern for partnership requires dying to ourselves and allowing God to craft our hearts in such a way that we do everything through his love. God is after people. To be an extension of his hands requires the grace one needs in order to love, which capacity is developed as God breaks us so we can be rebuilt to reflect all of him.

Joseph went to prison for a divine reason. Although the devil meant it for evil, God turned it around for good. For it was in prison that Joseph's skills and abilities were exposed. While confined, Joseph had more time to ponder on God and learn his heart. He also became a great listener, rather than speaking at the wrong time. Scripture notes that he was excellent at organizing and planning, so much so that the chief of the prison guards selected him for a new position as lead for the prisoners. Joseph's gift from God had been exposed. Known as the interpreter of dreams, he brought a whole new level of insight to the palace. It is in brokenness and challenges that the virtue in our hearts is exposed. Joseph's revelation of the seven years of famine and of the consequences of interpreting the baker's and cupbearer's dreams is a signal that Yahweh was beautifying the inner man of Joseph in his own way.

Another example of a broken person in scripture is Abraham. In Genesis 21:1–7 and Hebrews 6:15, we learn that he was considered by God to be a friend, which is indicative that friendship with God calls for us to be broken so that we may shed all the excesses that we carry and, in their stead, put on God's beauty. When God promised Abraham that he would make the number of his descendants as uncountable as the stars in the sky, it was a beautiful promise, but one that required Abraham to undergo the process of brokenness. Abraham only knew the outcome, which was the inheritance, but he had to learn to walk the path of brokenness, which would prepare him to handle his destiny. One must be trained to serve effectively as a CEO, a pilot, or a business tycoon or to take on any leadership position in life. Every profession and status in life has a school associated with it, along with both formal and informal education and hands-on training. So, it is with the kingdom of God. To effectively navigate the places where God has called you to be and has established you, you will require specific training; it is called the process of brokenness. Without brokenness, you are useless in the hands of God; you will limit his full potential from working in your life. It is like pouring water into a strainer, which is a waste of time and quite pointless.

In God's training school of brokenness, each person's training differs. And the rules are different based on one's assignment, character, and background. For instance, Abraham was already wealthy, so his training did not focus on how to obtain and maintain wealth. His training was focused on developing the perseverance to obtain the promise. This is of utmost significance to God; he makes adjustments to our characters so we may fully surrender as we go through the school of brokenness. He requires an excellent spirit, a distinct confidence in him, and action that reflects such confidence, which is faith. He also requires complete loyalty and trust regardless of what the visible world is indicating.

At the depth and core of brokenness is an intimacy that emerges as beautiful surrender. It is your brokenness that determines your usefulness to the kingdom of God. Until one is broken totally and yielded completely, one cannot be fruitful or useful in God's hands or be a vessel of honor.

Another biblical character who graduated from the school of brokenness is Daniel. We read in Daniel 6 that he had to get through this school of brokenness with his major concentration being loyalty and trust. Daniel's being unable to partake of the food on the king's table was a way of yielding himself completely to God for his assignment in Babylon. It looked like just another ordinary meal, but it was not, so this reflects Daniel's power of choice. Daniel could either continue serving Yahweh or choose the heathen god for the rest of his life in exile. We see how he continues to pray three times a day regardless of the decree of the lions' den. We see how he trusted God for the interpretation of King Darius's dream. All Daniel had was his trust in Yahweh. It was tested! The product of this particular process of brokenness influenced times and seasons, peoples, and nations. It extended to the turning over of decrees of the king. Daniel caused the king to recognize Yahweh, express his faith in Yahweh, and even change a decree that would lift the name of Yahweh in Babylon and point Babylonians to God's greatness. This is what the school of brokenness does: it points to Yahweh and brings him glory through the transformation of hearts, cities, nations, and governments.

As I walk the path of brokenness with lots of scars on my body and much thankfulness in my heart, I am able to see every road of challenge that the enemy plans to use as a hindrance to slow me down and wipe me out. This road plays right into God's hands as, through the process of brokenness, God turns hardship into beauty, setbacks into bridges to cross, and mistakes into opportunities for his name's sake and for his glory.

The journey of brokenness is not complete without total surrender, meaning that one must let go of what one believes one has a right to have and live a lifestyle of humility, trusting in the leadership of the Holy Spirit for direction. Thus, I draw strength and encouragement from those who have gone ahead of me and lived as a testament of brokenness to reflect beauty.

Chapter 6
The Bitter and the Sweet

I crossed lots of bridges and kept on going. I thought of the best things and, really, all the good things as I walked with God and waited on him. Nevertheless, there were more changes to occur as God continued to put me through this process. This stage of the process was much more complex because it took some time for me to realize the hand of God working within my life. It felt to me that another assignment was approaching.

I thought at the time that nothing else had been as painful as this new season. I had lost my husband, partner, and friend in an auto accident. It was very much unexpected. My wrist and elbow were broken in the wreck, and my oldest daughter's femur (thighbone) and talus (anklebone) were broken. I and my husband had been blessed with four kids. Our oldest daughter was seventeen. We had a pair of fraternal twins—a son and a daughter— who were nine, and an five-year-old son, who still resembles his dad. My late husband and I had had the dream of seeing our firstborn attend Oral Roberts University, and God was fulfilling that dream. I had been very excited as we prepared to take our daughter to College Weekend for her Whole Person Scholarship interview at Oral Roberts in Tulsa, Oklahoma. Unexpectedly, because of black ice on the bridge, we had a head-on collision with an eighteen-wheeler truck, which left my husband unconscious. Later he passed, after surgery. Interestingly, while on my way to one of my own surgeries, I was stopped by the doctor who was working on my husband, who wanted to reassure me that my husband's pulse was strong. After I woke up from surgery, my husband was gone.

Every victory has both a test and a process. On one hand, I was experiencing loss, and on the other hand I was experiencing great pain. My wristbone was broken and protruding out, disjointed, and my elbow was broken and had dislocated. Two surgeries with the use of plates and screws repaired these problems. And then there was my daughter, who was in unimaginable pain beyond description. She'd had to have her femur and talus repaired, followed by a rehabilitation period.

It was all fuzzy at first, but soon it became clear that my confusion was the result of loss, pain, and disappointment. This was not the first time in my life that things did not make sense to me. All these things were part of my brokenness journey. It was a weird kind of brokenness and preparation for the institution of Abba Father's purpose for my life and for movement in the direction in which he wished to take me. This was the worst kind of experience. It became a self-discovery journey, one where I sought to find my identity. I discovered that God wanted me to start all over again with a childlike faith, trusting in him in silent obedience as he built something beautiful in my life.

My life had made a 180-degree change. I was full of questions that I could not verbalize. I became unsure of myself and how to proceed, but still I did not let go of my grip. I held onto the love of God even though I could not process this entire season. It hurt a lot, but I always had an inner support. Now I understand that this is what is known as God's grace. I remember at St. Mary's Hospital in Russellville, Arkansas, where I, my husband, and our daughter had been treated, that we had had lots of help. One of the primary care nurses, Angel, was an actual angel in human form; she brought in her pastor's wife to sit with me until my friends and family could arrive in Arkansas. We were from Lawrenceville, Georgia. I remember how amazed she was when we were interacting; it was as if we had met each other before. It is called God's great grace, what I refer to as "the sweet." Angel had changed her shift just to stay with me and my daughter at the hospital. On top of that, she and her husband went to where our car had been wrecked and brought back everything they could salvage. You know that God was allowing me to experience his goodness and his confirmation that he was with me amid the loss and pain.

I made many unforgettable memories at the hospital, knowing that God was orchestrating events, which spoke to me of God's mercy and grace, nudging me to trust him with this season of my life. I had a met Angel, a kindhearted nurse the evening of my accident she had been assigned to my room. She was so moved by our circumstances that she asked her pastor's wife to visit with us. It was during the second day of her visit that I experience something unusual; a case of God's grace when a stranger walked into my hospital room, left something on the table, and left. I had seen only the back of the person as he or she was leaving the room. I looked at the table. Seeing that the object left behind was a book. It was the manual that the Lord was going to use to speak to me every morning and evening to come. That experience was so real … so real! It's amazing how the Holy Spirit allowed me simply to give myself to Sarah Young's devotional *Jesus Calling: Enjoying Peace in His Presence*. My edition featured a beautiful baby-pink cover, which made me smile deeply. It is funny how much it amused me to roll over every morning and evening, looking forward to that visitation from Jesus. It was one of the highlights of my day hearing and knowing what God wanted me to do for that day. Believe me, it brought sweetness to my day. It brought strength to me knowing that God still held my hands.

The bittersweet experiences I'd been through all had to do with where God was taking me. Being elevated is like getting a promotion. Some people experience double promotion, which they you skip a class and enroll in an advanced course, which really looks good on one's transcript. Some people are just promoted to accelerated classes; others simply take the normal route. But for me, this occurrence felt like a double promotion, meaning I had to take accelerated classes. I experienced God in a very pure, childlike manner. I was very clear on my instructions. I learned to forget about the classes I had taken, and I discovered that I had two choices: either stay in prison to my demise or learn the other side of God and take hold of my promises.

I followed the pathway to promise within the prison walls. I learned to trust God again, taking baby steps to get my life back on track. It was very difficult because my emotions were wounded. I increased my worship, which helped me surrender more to God. I asked God to help me, heal my heart, rescue me, and deliver me. The Holy Spirit began to heal my heart and give me rest. As I got some rest, I trusted God more and realized I had to get on with my life. God started to open doors of opportunity for me. Things that God once had spoken in my heart and through his people were reinstated and reminded me again of "Through the mouths of prophets and apostles …»

Chapter 7
The Fun Side of Brokenness: God's Faithfulness

Believe it or not, there is a fun side to brokenness that is much preferred to the side that is not much fun at all. This fun side is God's constant reminders to you that he is with you and he is in charge regardless of the challenges you are confronted with. The opposite side involves the reminder that this is a dry season, a desert season, but a season of promise. It is a season of disappointment yet of feeling the love of the Father. It is a season of frustration but also a season of total dependence on God. It is a period of leaving the known for the unknown, because what you know becomes irrelevant and unnecessary. It becomes a period of learning to trust God all over again. It is the time you engage your childlike faith. The trials are much more tedious and constant. The barrage positions you to trust in God and love him or face despair. It also a season to make new discoveries in God and to rest in him.

It was a challenge to me, the resting session. I have always been a busy bee. I do not even consider taking naps; whenever I try, I wake up suddenly after fifteen minutes, thinking I am wasting time sleeping. However, God taught me how to enter into rest even with everything in my life out of order, with lots of bills to pay, and with everything running dry.

It was a new thing for me to rest assuredly in God and not try to use my own strategies to fix things. It was very difficult, but during this journey of brokenness, I was to rest on the wings of the Holy Spirit and let him order and fix things no matter that my life was spinning out of control. Indeed, this was a journey of resting and trusting.

Furthermore, the fun side is letting the Holy Spirit do his perfect work, which involves smoothing the rough edges of your life. Brokenness brings a smoothness, making it easier for God to walk with you. Walking with God is part of the fun side of being broken. Enoch walked with God and as a result pleased God (Hebrews 11:5). Because his connection with God was pleasing to God, he did not taste death but was transported to another dimension, where he remained with God not only physically but also spiritually. Walking with God in the season of brokenness becomes a necessity. The real benefit of this season is that you get to experience intimacy with God, trusting him as your newfound lover and pleasing him. It is a phase we all must go through as we are in the state of brokenness to be made anew.

This phase sparks a purpose for living and for understanding one's journey with God. It gives clear direction and purifies one's motive; being childlike and purer yet simultaneously being oneself is what this season demands.

As I waited on the Lord to heal me and restore me after my husband's death, I was miserable not being able to figure anything out or use my own strategies to find answers. All I did was surrender, trusting in God and depending on him totally. I started a fresh walk with God, waiting eagerly for him to speak to me every morning and throughout the day when I was by myself. I had been married for nineteen years and nine months; losing my husband, my friend, my kids' father, was a shock. I felt as if time had stopped. I had no explanation for why this has happened. My pain was both physical and emotional.

The vacuum I experienced caused me to turn to God more than I had ever done before, instead of being bitter, offended, closed off, and depressed. I ran to God with everything, and I was willing to trust him through this phase. The songs I had been singing to worship the Lord began to make more sense; the things they addressed had become my reality. Take for instance Kari Jobe's song "I Am Not Alone" ("You are not alone. You will go before me. You will never leave me …") and William McDowell's "I Give Myself Away" ("I give myself away so you can use me. … My life is not my own. To you I belong …"). Since worship has always been a big part of my life, I accessed the love of the Father through that means amid my discomfort and pain.

The accident was one thing, but my difficulties were the posttraumatic effects. I needed to run to God and his supernatural higher power. What was the assignment he had in mind, and why had he chosen this time? I had never wondered about this before, but as I came more and more into God's presence, I realized that nothing had been about me; everything was all for his glory. Having to combat challenges in so many forms and shapes was a sort of preparation to becoming the refined vessel God wanted me to be. It is a necessary evil one must endure to accomplish God's purpose.

To be in brokenness is an uncomfortable place. No one would desire to be broken, but it is a good place to be. It communicates that one is getting into shape and being worked on by God himself. You see, this state of brokenness is the only place where you get to appeal to God's compassion and emotion (Psalm 34:18). Since to be broken and rebuilt is one way of beautifying our image, it must occur. It uproots us and transplants us in the places we ought to be according to God's plan for us. Isaiah 28:8 confirms that at this point, our light will break forth. That light comes out of our brokenness. It is the dawn of another season of life, which means everything is brand new. It is at this time that healing will occur, and your righteousness will go forth like the dawn. These things only happen when brokenness has taken place.

Chapter 8
Fulfillment and Bliss

This next phase is the phase marked by the unstoppable and overwhelming love that we experience as we go through God's school of brokenness. It is an experience of understanding God's love and receiving it from the author of life, Christ Jesus. I experienced God's love as being so thick that I could not go through it; he had to make it go through me because he *is* love. Amid the terror, tragedies, and disappointment without end that one feels once one has been enrolled in the school of brokenness, a precious treasure of great value that has heretofore been hiding inside one is released.

I discovered that I started to find fulfillment and enjoy bliss as the storm passed and a new season opened to me. This is where I found God as the expert who sets the stage and orders everything in this season. One navigates this season with total surrender, love, and obedience, all these having been birthed from the journey brokenness. I began to live for God's assignments and purpose. As I went from bliss toward fulfillment, I still had disappointments that changed my life's purpose. However, being enrolled in the school of brokenness required that I give Jesus full control of my life, meaning that he has the prerogative to interrupt my seasons, create moments, and establish his loving purpose for my life.

I plugged into knowing God's heart. This change led me to seek God more fervently and to be dependent on his grace during the most difficult seasons of my life. A lot of my friends had abandoned me, so I'd become content to depend on God and to hold on to his promises. I realized it was either that I fall in love with Jesus beyond myself or I fail to emerge from that season. I saw myself as being subject to a sacred process of brokenness, holding onto the promise like Abraham moving from tent to tent, although he carried the promise he was looking for, namely, a city whose maker and builder was God. Even more I realized I was been molded for an unusual assignment. All the years I had been in the presence of God, I had never felt this way with him before. He showed the greatest depths of his personality. It was overwhelming, overpowering, in a good way. He strategically put certain warriors into my life. It was as if I were on a strict diet, not allowed to eat any unhealthy food or have any snacks.

I moved on, allowing God to work through me. God opened the door to my career. In fact, I got one of the finest jobs available after I'd learned of a career opportunity. What I am saying is that the process of brokenness does not make sense to the human mind because of the rigorous path one has to walk. Nevertheless, the wisdom of God is foolishness in the eyes of carnal humankind. God began to open doors of opportunity so I could get the training I would need for my career. He also opened the door to travel, where I got to experience other environments with both God and people. God will let you go to great depths with him, almost in another dimension, when you submit to his will. Thank you, Jesus, because the process is beautiful; through it, I am being made beautiful. And I feel beautiful in God's hands, even though I have many scars to remind me of my path of brokenness. Actually, it is ongoing; it doesn't stop until God ushers you into that place of divine assignment, which is always seasonal.

Chapter 9
The Assignment

Your assignment is God's ultimate purpose and objective for your life. What does this mean? You will discover soon enough that none of us are on earth without a purpose. My senior pastor uses the illustration that when babies are born, they come out of their mothers' wombs with their hands closed. He notes that babies are holding on to the divine assignment they have for here on earth. It is an interesting scenario, which makes me wonder what was in my hands as I emerged into this world. Well, from the look of things, it seems that I had a firm grip on my assignment.

Perceptibly, it appears that our assignment is the primary purpose for our existence. You might be thinking, *I was born for great things, perhaps to change the world, influence systems or governments, dominate the business world, or affect the financial industry or the entertainment world, but I was not cut out for this Jesus thing. I was not born to be preaching on the pulpit, and I have none of the fivefold ministry giftings.* If you are thinking such things, then know that I understand you and agree with you. But your assignment is your calling, the place where God has planted you. It is a place where God is taking you and sometimes may be a place where you have already been. There is an influence that you carry; it is God-breathed. It makes you versatile in your area of calling. There is also an spirit of excellence attached to that calling of, say, problem-solving and being innovative. It is a calling; it is your assignment. How you perform in your assignment is crucial to your destiny. How you allow the breath of God to fully manifest into a specific assignment for you determines what heights you will reach in God's kingdom.

Assignments vary; every person possesses diverse callings depending upon their destiny. So, whether your assignments are of great significance or are just mediocre or low-key, they are very much connected to your survival.

God may have given you an assignment in the financial world so that nothing in the world of finance has the power to overwhelm you. You show your expertise with numbers, you understand the complexities of the stock market, you are an expert at negotiation, and when it comes to finance, you show great knowledge about the most profitable ways of trading. This has been your interest, and it speaks to you. I want you to note that it is not an interest; it's more of an innate ability that is being expressed. When you press further in this line of work toward developing yourself, to become an expert in those specific areas, then your calling manifests.

The types of callings vary in all careers and giftings. It is our gifts and our talents that we use as our resources to develop a career. The world calls it a profession, a job, or an occupation, but it is a calling and divine assignment that has already been determined by God—"For without me you can do nothing" (John 15:5).

Certainly, CEOs, bank managers, financial managers, businesspeople, and so forth all have received callings. Such people start flourishing with the gifts of leadership and expertise in implementing their knowledge of a certain subject matter, but this all goes toward the calling. Given this phenomenon, we are charged with the responsibility of exhibiting the initiative to carry out our divine assignment. We were created for this assignment. One of God's plans for humanity was to restore the human race to its rightful position with the blood of Jesus, freeing us from the hands of the devil, so we could be his voice, be his hands and his feet, and manifest him in his kingdom here on earth.

Remarkably, I thought I had been saved so I could live a wonderful Christian life with my family and simply have a victorious hallelujah type of life. This was my perception as a believer. Nevertheless, I was predestined to live out the existence God had planned for me. We are all born into our assignment. I was born into my assignment, which I could not discover because I had a Gideon mentality. I was very much afraid without any idea of where this fear originated from. Whatever its source, it was sure having its way with my life. It was the greatest stumbling block I encountered, preventing me from beginning to carry out my assignment. It deterred me from maximizing my full potential, but in the end it didn't win. I had been fully equipped and enabled before I was born for this assignment, which involved advancing the kingdom of God.

You are advancing the kingdom of God simply by being in your role and functioning. But your assignment does not include being sidetracked, becoming preoccupied with irrelevancies, or functioning poorly. One's assignment will always be twofold, functioning in the secular realm and the spiritual realm simultaneously. But most of the time people end up manifesting in just one realm because they have failed to associate their assignment with God, instead believing that their own ability has earned them their position and status. It is not so; every assignment that God has ever given a human being is to advance the kingdom of God here on earth. Regardless of the nature of the assignment, it affects God's purpose. I am totally aware of the devil's assignment too, but since *Broken for Assignment* is about the assignments of God, I will not comment on the issue.

My assignment is focused on the seven motivational gifts that are highlighted in Romans 12:7–8, as follows: "If your gift is that of serving others, serve them well. If you are a teacher, do a good job of teaching. If you are a preacher, see to it that your sermons are strong and helpful. If God has given you money, be generous in helping others with it. If God has given you administrative ability and put you in charge of the work of others, take the responsibility seriously. Those who offer comfort to the sorrowing should do so with Christian cheer" (TLB).

There are seven categories of job tasks that apply to non-faith-based jobs and faith-based jobs. "They are perceiving, serving, teaching, encouraging, giving, ruling, and mercy."[1] Interestingly, this is the underlying feature of all the job descriptions and all career paths. With this in mind, you might see why being broken is necessary if one is to do these assignments excellently, using God's methods and accomplishing his purpose. This is the place where the simultaneous twofold assignment is appropriate. God must process each of us so that we may come to uncompromisingly accomplish his task. Submitting to this process does not feel as pleasant as it may sound.

Now, I am fully aware that we are an extension of God here on earth and that he does take his purposes seriously. He is not a discriminatory Father; he spontaneously supports each of us with his heart as we carry out our assignments. His love for us is unconditional. It is what motivates us to carry out the assignments in our lives. As he uses me in these tasks, I feel the need to bring his kingdom here to earth. Consequently, I have a need for

---

[1] Bruce E. Winston, "The Romans 12 Gifts: Useful for Person–Job Fit," *Journal of Biblical Perspectives in Leadership* 2, no. 2 (Summer 2009): 114–34.

God to process me so I may align myself to his purpose and fully understand my assignment. Me and Christ, the holy and anointed one do have the same objective; it is called imparting and transforming.

I speak to all the precious hearts who are reading a copy of *Broken for Assignment* today. There must be a reason the Holy Spirit allowed you to pick up this book to read. He is speaking to you directly about your assignment. Wanting to give you a clearer understanding of the path you are walking, he desires to realign your heart with his purpose so you may best carry out your assignment. Listen, any time, resources, or strength you invest in your assignment is only valuable when it has been processed by God. Surrender yourself and submit to God's processing, as this will guarantee a greater harvest.

Thus, the journey of *Broken for Assignment*, when looked at perceptively, points to a very intimate love story between God and humanity. He waters, prunes, and tends the plant so it may be fruitful. He refashions us so we may be perfect in him.

Praise for Broken for Assignment

I'm speaking from the perspective of wife and partner in ministry to the general overseer of ANCFC, and also as mother to all the children from many nations of the globe whom God has put in my loins.

It's so amazing to witness how God use the issues of life to keep us on the right track, pointing us toward the finish line as we run the race as disciples.

Seeing what God is doing with my spiritual daughter Lorna gives me the desire to do more for God. She is a daughter who will say yes to the assignment in spite of any pains and trials.

I believe that her story will help you see that God will use anything to get your attention and refocus your heart so you may come to know the purpose of your existence here on earth. *Broken for Assignment* will help you understand your assignments as a child of God and will enlighten you to the place where God is taking you.

Dr. Nathalie Mukwiza
Pastor at ANCFC, United Nations Ambassador, Fashion Designer, Founder of the NC Boutique

As an educator, I have the privilege of seeing many vessels at different stages, precious jewels who have not recognized what they truly carry. "It is ruined." I can't do it!" "It won't work." Who told you such things?

Most times, we do not know the true worth or value of a thing or a person until you see the thing or person in a broken state. Brokenness comes in many forms and never seems to be pleasant. Jesus had to be broken to the point of death so that salvation may be available to all. His body being broken from the whips and the crown of thorns, along with him being nailed to the cross, allowed for healing in every area. I do not know where you are. You may be in a place where you are shattered into pieces. You may be in a place of apathy. Or perhaps you are observing someone who is in that place. I encourage you to travel through the pages of *Broken for Assignment* as beauty is on the horizon.

Mrs. Pheletta Kayea, Senior Faculty, Archer High School;
worship leader, ANCFC, Lawrenceville, Georgia, USA

When I met Pastor Lorna . for the first time. I pondered in my heart how a woman could have passion for the kingdom of God like this. It did not take long time for me to discover that she was indeed a special anointed women of God who love the lord and who God has granted wisdom and understanding far beyond her natural years in the lord.

She's a hard working women of God behind the scene. Everything that God made valuable in the world is covered and hard to get to.

Where do you find diamonds?

Deep in the ground, covered and protected. Where do you find pearls?

Deep down at the bottom of the ocean, covered up and protected in a beautiful shell.

Where do you find gold?

Way down in mine, covered with layers and layers of rock you've got to work hard to get them

God looks at you with precious eyes you're far more precious than gold and diamonds and pearls and you should be covered as well. (Proverbs 3:15).

God has a plan with your future you're a blessing for next generation

I recommend that you read this book and share with your friends

God bless you.

his Excellency Rev Dr Moses Mukwiza
UN Ambassador at large to Vienna.

Printed in the United States
by Baker & Taylor Publisher Services